FRED FLIPS!

Dedicated to Tom Fontecchio, who recognized my potential and provided every opportunity to help me achieve my dreams. Your support and care made me feel at home in a world where I felt different.

Also dedicated to my parents, whose unwavering confidence and positivity inspired me throughout my athletic journey.

Text copyright © 2025 by Frederick Richard and Ryan G. Van Cleave

Illustrations copyright © 2025 by Darcie Olley

Published by Bushel & Peck Books, a family-run publishing house in Fresno, California, who believes in uplifting children with the highest standards of art, music, literature, and ideas. For every book we sell, we donate one to a child in need—book for book. To nominate a school or organization to receive free books, or to find inspiring books and gifts, please visit www.bushelandpeckbooks.com.

All rights reserved. No part of this publication may be reproduced without written permission from the publisher.

Type set in Temeraire and Rafaella.

LCCN: 2024947539

ISBN: 978-1-63819-229-9

First Edition

Printed in Canada

1 3 5 7 9 10 8 6 4 2

FRED FLIPS!

HOW ONE GYMNAST REALIZED THAT DIFFERENCES CAN BECOME STRENGTHS

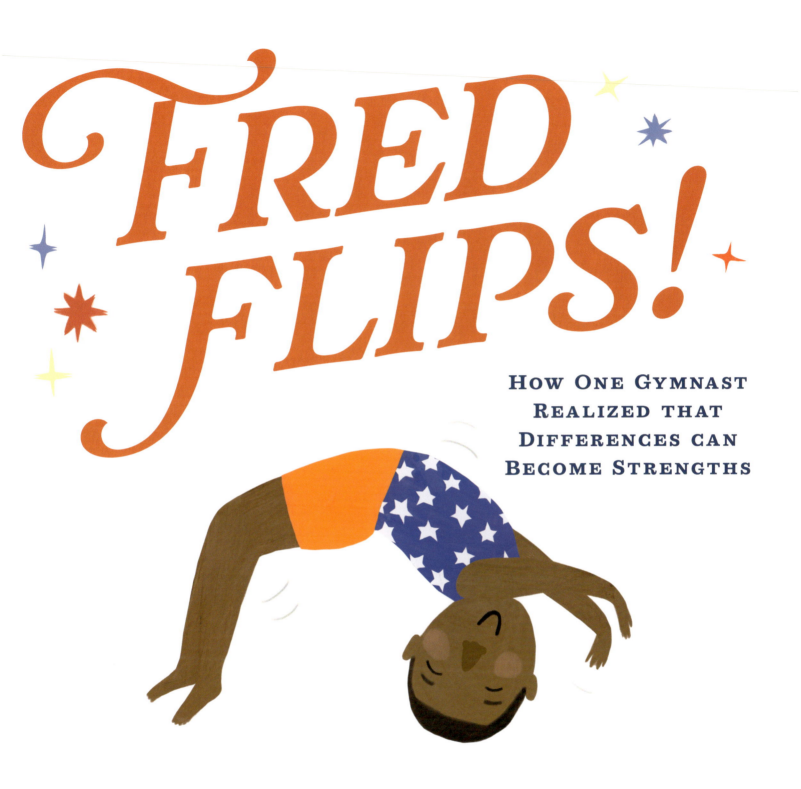

By Olympic Medalist **FREDERICK RICHARD**
WITH RYAN G. VAN CLEAVE

Illustrated by **DARCIE OLLEY**

BUSHEL
& PECK
BOOKS

Fred Richard always felt the *FLIPS* inside him. Even before he could talk, he was flipping in his crib, giggling as his parents watched in awe.

"THIS BOY'S GOT GYMNASTICS IN HIS BONES!"

As Fred grew older, his flips got bigger and better. He tumbled on the couch, jumped off the bed, and spun in the yard. Gymnastics wasn't just fun—it was what Fred was meant to do.

But when he started going to the gym, something felt off. Most of the gymnasts were girls. Fred was a boy. And not just any boy—he was a boy with skin so black that even his friends joked one night, "Where's Fred? He's disappeared into the dark!"

Fred just shrugged and joked, "I'm practicing my ninja skills!" But inside, he wondered if people would ever truly accept him for who he was.

No matter how hard he tried to fit in, Fred always stood out. His skin was darker, his muscles stronger, and his flips **WILDER**.

At a family cookout, Fred's dad hit the dance floor with goofy moves. His big, confident smile soon had everyone twirling and laughing along with him.

Later, he grinned at Fred. "Why just fit in when you can *SHINE*?"

That was it. Simple, clear. Fred realized it was possible to stand out and still belong.

The next day at the gym, Fred was practicing when someone whispered, "Where's Fred? He's vanished into the mats!"

Fred squared his shoulders. "You might not see me now," he said, "but you'll definitely see me on the podium!"

The gym went quiet. Fred's heart pounded, but he felt a sense of relief. Slowly, he began to stand a little taller.

From then on, Fred decided to **FLIP** the script, literally. He worked for more than medals. Every flip sent his heart soaring, and that was all the motivation he needed.

He pushed harder,

flipped higher,

and practiced longer.

Fred focused on what made gymnastics amazing.

BALANCE.

Strength.

Flexibility.

And every time he felt different, he reminded himself: "Different is *GOOD*. Different is *STRONG*."

But when the Future Stars Nationals loomed ahead, Fred's nerves hit harder than ever. He was about to face his first *BIG* competition. If he made the team, he'd head to the Olympic training center.

                                         If not . . .

The night before the event, Fred lay awake, his chest tight like he was gripping the still rings, fighting to hold steady under the pressure.

On competition day, bright lights filled the arena. As he stepped onto the mat, Fred felt everyone's eyes on him. Then the crowd began to whisper. But Fred didn't listen.

AND HE DID!

Fred's flips were sharper, his landings stronger. He wasn't just competing—he was *FLYING*. With every twist and turn, he showed everyone that his differences weren't something to hide. They were his *SUPERPOWERS*.

When the scores were posted, Fred felt a rush of joy. He'd given his all and flown higher than ever. But was it enough?

He scanned the list . . . and his heart skipped a beat.

HE'D MADE IT!

As he stepped onto the podium, Fred felt more than pride. He felt like he truly belonged. For the first time, it didn't matter how different he seemed, or what anyone had whispered or joked. He wasn't just a name on the list. He was a gymnast who had earned his place.

Fred stood *TALL*, knowing his journey wasn't about fitting in—it was about standing out. He hoped every kid watching would remember that their differences could be their greatest strength, in and out of the gym.

Over the noise of the cheering crowd, Fred heard a familiar voice shout from the stands, "THIS BOY'S GOT GYMNASTICS IN HIS BONES. JUST LOOK AT HIM SHINE!"

Fred smiled. He knew he'd been shining all along.

About Frederick "Flips" Richard

Olympic gymnast Frederick Richard is a World All-Around Bronze Medalist and reigning NCAA Men's All-Around Champion who took the world by storm at the 2024 Paris Olympics. Fred has been named to the 2024 TIME100 Next list, which highlights one hundred emerging leaders who are shaping the future of business, entertainment, sports, politics, health, science, activism, and more. He is a student at the University of Michigan in Ann Arbor and a native of Stoughton, Massachusetts.

About Ryan G. Van Cleave

Ryan G. Van Cleave wrote his first poem at age five, and he's been writing, reading, and loving poetry ever since. He earned a PhD in American literature with an emphasis in poetry and has taught at numerous colleges and universities. As the Picture Book Doctor, he helps celebrities write stories for kids and bring them to life on the page, stage, and screen. He lives in Florida.

About Darcie Olley

Darcie Olley is an illustrator based in the east of England. She uses a mixture of acrylic, watercolor, gouache, pencil, and digital techniques in her work to create illustrations full of vibrancy, humor, and joy. Darcie's work is often inspired by her Indian heritage, her love for animals (you can often find her trying to make friends with the neighborhood cats), and the funny and simple little things she notices about day-to-day life!